Union Public Library
1980 Morris Avenue
Union, N.J. 07083

P9-DLZ-392

Looking Closely

in the

Rain Forest

Union Public Library
1980 Morris Avenue
Union, N.J. 07083

FRANK SERAFINI

Kids Can Press

Look very closely.

What do you see?

Sand dunes?
Pussy willow?
What could it be?

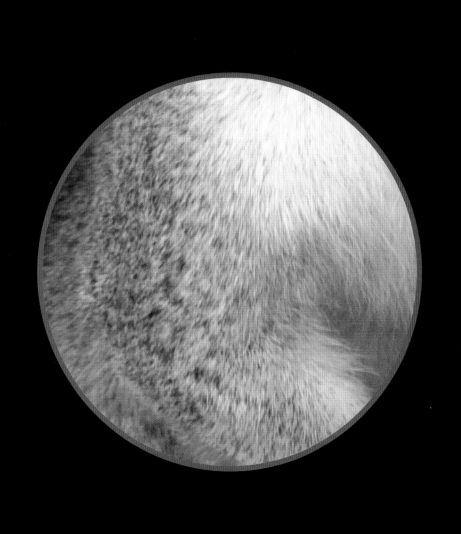

It's a *Squirrel* Monkey.

Squirrel monkeys are named for their small size and the fact that they live in trees. You can spot one by looking for black eyes in a white mask. Squirrel monkeys live in large groups. In the evenings, you can hear them chattering in the trees.

Unlike some monkeys, squirrel monkeys use their tails to balance on tree limbs, not for climbing. They run along tree branches and leap from one tree to another.

Look very closely.

What do you see?

A flamingo?
Pink grapefruit?
What could it be?

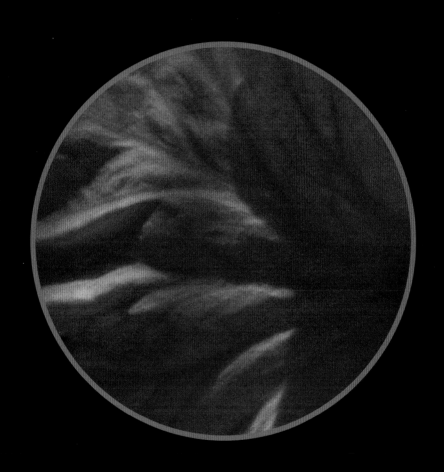

It's a
Hibiscus.

These brightly colored flowers are hard to miss in the rain forest. They come in many colors, including red, white, yellow, pink and purple. Each plant produces dozens of flowers.

Hibiscus flowers bloom for only one day. When the sun comes out in the morning, the trumpet-shaped flowers open their petals wide to soak up the sun's energy.

Look very closely.

What do you see?

A spaceship?
A sea slug?
What could it be?

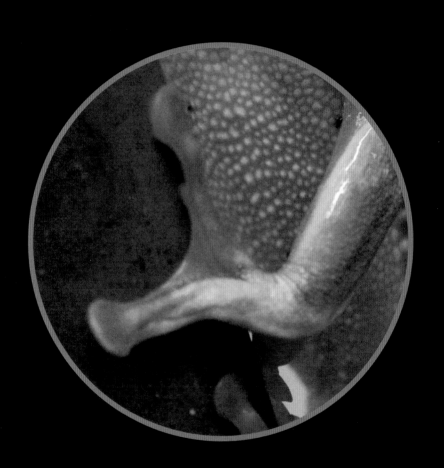

It's a Red-Eyed Tree Frog.

It's easy to see where red-eyed tree frogs get their name. Their bulging red eyes scare off snakes, birds and bats looking for a meal. Red-eyed tree frogs also have suction cups on their toes — perfect for clinging to branches and climbing up and down trees.

Red-eyed tree frogs are nocturnal. This means that they hunt for insects at night and sleep during the day.

Look very closely.

What do you see?

Hot peppers?
Goblin fingers?
What could it be?

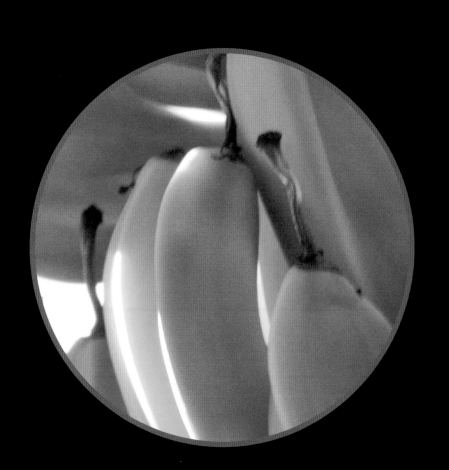

It's a Banana Plant.

Bananas start out green and turn yellow or red as they ripen. These tasty fruits grow in bunches. Each banana is called a finger.

Bananas grow on the world's largest flowering plant. The banana plant is so large it looks like a tree. Its leaves can grow up to 3 m (9 ft.) long. In some countries, people use banana leaves as umbrellas.

Look very closely.

What do you see?

Chestnuts?
Sea coral?
What could it be?

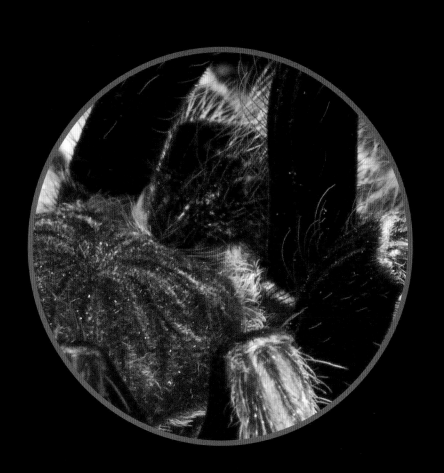

It's a Zebra Tarantula.

Tarantulas are large, hairy spiders. They have eight legs, and each leg has a claw on the end used for climbing. This spider is called a zebra tarantula because of its black-and-white fur.

Tarantulas do not spin webs. Instead, some use their silk to line their burrows. Tarantulas hunt for food. They mainly feed on insects, but some tarantulas will eat mice, frogs and small lizards.

Look very closely.

What do you see?

A piñata?
A parachute?
What could it be?

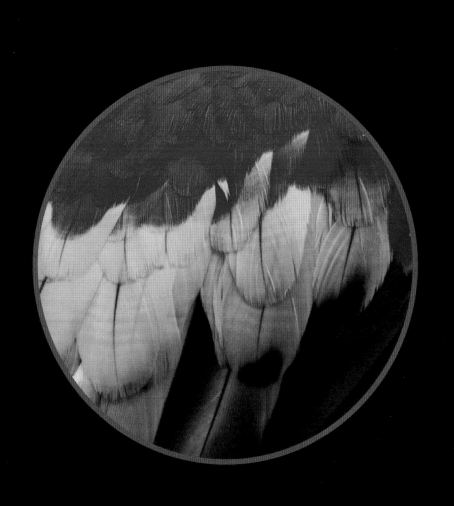

It's a *Scarlet* Macaw.

Scarlet macaws are a type of parrot. These brightly colored birds live in the highest tree branches of the rain forest, called the canopy. They use their powerful beaks to crack open hard shells and feed on fruits, seeds and nuts.

Scarlet macaws usually travel in pairs or small groups. They can be very noisy, and their screeches and calls can carry for kilometers (miles).

Look very closely.

What do you see?

A xylophone?
A picket fence?
What could it be?

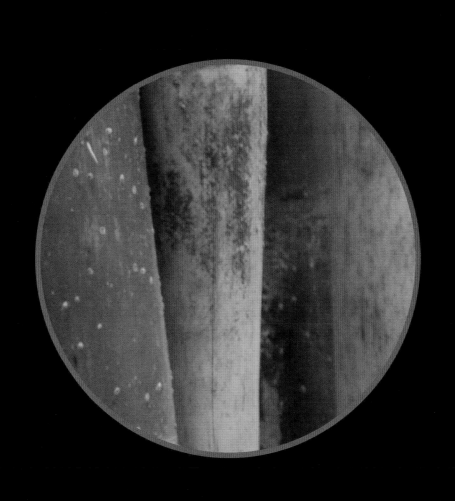

It's Bamboo.

Bamboo is the largest type of grass in the world. It can grow over 30 m (100 ft.) high. That's taller than a two-story house! It is also the fastest growing plant in the world. Some kinds of bamboo can grow more than 1 m (3 ft.) in one day.

Bamboo is used for making many things, from toothpicks to houses. It is also used for food. Pandas love to eat bamboo. People eat young bamboo plants, called shoots.

Look very closely.

What do you see?

An alien?
A seahorse?
What could it be?

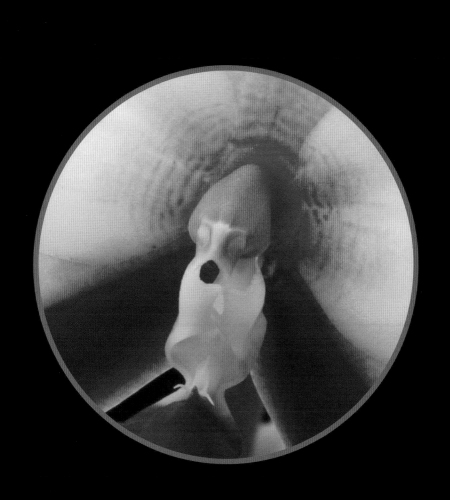

It's a Moth Orchid.

There are over 30 000 different types of orchids in the world. This orchid is named for its petals, which look like moth wings. When a moth orchid blooms, its flowers will last for several weeks at a time.

Orchids love shady, warm and humid places. This is why they thrive in many of the world's rain forests. These colorful plants can grow on rocks, creep over the ground and even climb up trees.

Look very closely.

What do you see?

Sandpaper?
Fish teeth?
What could it be?

It's a *Spiny-Tailed* Iguana.

Spiny-tailed iguanas get their name from the spines that run down their backs and tails. These large lizards eat mostly flowers and fruits, although they will sometimes feed on small animals and eggs.

The spiny-tailed iguana is one of the fastest lizards in the world. It can run up to 33 km (20 mi.) per hour! More commonly, spiny-tailed iguanas can be found sitting atop large rocks or fallen tree branches and basking in the warm sun.

This book is dedicated to my daughter, Nicole, and my grandson, Vaughn. My life is much richer with you in it. Many new adventures lie ahead.

Photographer's Note

Photographers pay attention to things that most people overlook or take for granted. I can spend hours wandering outdoors in my favorite places looking for interesting things to photograph. My destination is not actually a place, but rather a new way of seeing.

It takes time to notice things. To be a photographer, you have to slow down and imagine in your "mind's eye" what the camera can capture. Ansel Adams said you could discover a whole life's worth of images in a six-square-foot patch of Earth. In order to do so, you have to look very closely.

By creating the images featured in this series of picture books, I hope to help people attend to nature, to things they might have normally passed by. I want people to pay attention to the world around them, to appreciate what nature has to offer, and to begin to protect the fragile environment in which we live.

Text and photographs © 2010 Frank Serafini

Pages 38–39: Taveuni, Fiji   Back cover: Daintree rain forest, Australia

All rights reserved. No part of this publication may be reproduced, stored in a retrieval system or transmitted, in any form or by any means, without the prior written permission of Kids Can Press Ltd. or, in case of photocopying or other reprographic copying, a license from The Canadian Copyright Licensing Agency (Access Copyright). For an Access Copyright license, visit www.accesscopyright.ca or call toll free to 1-800-893-5777.

Kids Can Press acknowledges the financial support of the Government of Ontario, through the Ontario Media Development Corporation's Ontario Book Initiative.

Published in Canada by
Kids Can Press Ltd.
29 Birch Avenue
Toronto, ON M4V 1E2

Published in the U.S. by
Kids Can Press Ltd.
2250 Military Road
Tonawanda, NY 14150

www.kidscanpress.com

Edited by Karen Li
Designed by Julia Naimska

This book is smyth sewn casebound.
Manufactured in Tseung Kwan O, Kowloon, Hong Kong, China, in 3/2010 by Paramount Printing Co. Ltd.

CM 10 0 9 8 7 6 5 4 3 2 1

Library and Archives Canada Cataloguing in Publication

Serafini, Frank
Looking closely in the rain forest / Frank Serafini.

(Looking closely)
Ages 3 to 7.
ISBN 978-1-55337-543-2

1. Rain forests—Juvenile literature.
2. Photography, Close-up. I. Title.
II. Series: Looking closely (Toronto, Ont.)

QH86.S474 2010   j578.734   C2009-906581-9

σ 6|12

Kids Can Press is a **LOrus**™ Entertainment company